Dr. GOLDILOCKS and the THREE BEARS' THYROIDS

EDWARD GALE MOVIUS, MD

ILLUSTRATED BY KAYLA V. BYRNES

DEDICATION:

To my father, William Robert Movius, MD, and my grandfather, Arthur James Movius, MD, who taught me the importance of compassionate patient communication, and to my wife, Therese Brendler, PhD, for her loving encouragement.

When Goldilocks was a little girl, she visited the home of the Three Bears. She ate their porridge, sat in their chairs, and tried to sleep in their beds. She found that Papa Bear's bed was too hard, Mama Bear's bed was too soft, and Baby Bear's bed was just right. She fell asleep in Baby Bear's bed but awoke suddenly when the Three Bears came home.

When she last saw them, she told them that she was going away to school.

Goldilocks graduated from high school, went to college, and then went to medical school to become a doctor.

After Dr. Goldilocks finished her training as a medical intern and resident, she completed a fellowship in endocrinology to learn about hormones that circulate in our blood and control many of our body processes.

She became an endocrinologist so that she could help bears and other animals that have diabetes and problems with their thyroid glands, their adrenal glands, and their pituitary glands.

She decided to open her office near the Three Bears' home.

One day the Three Bears came to her office because they felt sick.

The first bear that Dr. Goldilocks saw was Mama Bear.

"How do you feel?" Dr. Goldilocks asked Mama Bear.

Mama Bear said, "I don't feel well.
I've gained a lot of weight. I feel cold all the time.

I sleep much more than I used to.

My fur is dry and coarse. My face is puffy.

I feel all stopped up. I don't have enough energy to do my work."

Dr. Goldilocks said, "Let me examine you and try to figure out what is wrong with you."

Dr. Goldilocks examined Mama Bear.

She looked into Mama Bear's eyes, ears, and mouth.

She listened to her heart and lungs.

She felt her legs.

She also examined Mama Bear's thyroid at the base of her neck.

Dr. Goldilocks said, "Your thyroid is large, and it feels lumpy.

We need to do some blood tests and a thyroid ultrasound to help us figure out what is wrong with you."

Mama Bear went to the lab, and Dr. Goldilocks drew a sample of her blood.

Dr. Goldilocks then measured the amount of thyroid hormone in the bear's blood and the amount of thyroid stimulating hormone, the brain hormone that stimulates the thyroid to make thyroid hormone.

She also measured antibodies against the thyroid that are in some bears' blood. She explained that antibodies in bears' blood usually fight infections caused by viruses and bacteria, but some antibodies can cause the thyroid gland to produce too much or not enough thyroid hormone.

Dr. Goldilocks then examined Mama Bear's thyroid with an ultrasound machine.

The ultrasound uses sound waves to make a picture of the bear's thyroid.

She told Mama Bear, "You have several small lumps in your thyroid."

Mama Bear came back to see Dr. Goldilocks when the results of the blood tests were ready.

Dr. Goldilocks said, "I know what is wrong with you. Your thyroid is not making enough thyroid hormone.

Antibodies in your blood are causing your thyroid to make less thyroid hormone than it should.

We call this HYPOTHYROIDISM."

"What can you do to make me feel better?" asked Mama Bear.

Dr. Goldilocks said, "We will give you a pill that has some extra thyroid hormone in it.

If you take this pill every day, you will feel better in a few weeks."

Mama Bear went to the pharmacy to get her thyroid pills.

Then she went home and took one pill every day.

After four weeks she went back to see Dr. Goldilocks.

"How do you feel now?" asked Dr. Goldilocks.

"I feel so much better," she said.
"I am not gaining weight anymore.
I am not cold anymore.

I have more energy to work and play.
And my hair and fur are not dry anymore."

Dr. Goldilocks said to her, "It sounds like your thyroid hormone level is exactly where it should be:

Not too **LOW**, not too **HIGH**, but **JUST RIGHT**."

The next day, Dr. Goldilocks saw Baby Bear and asked, "How are you feeling today?"

"I haven't been feeling right for the past few weeks," said Baby Bear.

"I always feel hot.

I have lost weight.
I eat more but am still losing weight.

My heart is pounding all the time.
My paws shake all the time.

My hair and fur are falling out.

I have to go to the bathroom more often.

I also have trouble sleeping."

Dr. Goldilocks said, "Let me examine you. I'll try to figure out what is wrong with you."

Dr. Goldilocks examined Baby Bear.

She looked into Baby Bear's eyes, ears, and mouth.
She listened to her heart and lungs.

She felt her legs.
She also examined Baby Bear's thyroid.

Dr. Goldilocks said, "Your thyroid is bigger than it should be.
Your heart is going faster than it should.

I also see that your paws shake when you hold out your arms.

We need to do a blood test and an ultrasound of your neck to help us figure out what is wrong with you."

Dr. Goldilocks used the ultrasound to look at Baby Bear's neck and thyroid.

She said, "Your thyroid is very large and has lots of blood flowing through it.

It is shaped like a big butterfly."

Baby Bear went to the laboratory and then came back to see Dr. Goldilocks when the results of the blood tests were ready.

Dr. Goldilocks said, "I know what is wrong with you.

Your thyroid is making much more thyroid hormone than it should.

You have antibodies in your blood that are causing the thyroid to make the extra hormone.

We call this condition HYPERTHYROIDISM.

Here are some pills called methimazole. This medicine will cause your thyroid gland to make less thyroid hormone and make you feel better.

You should take them every day and come back in two weeks."

Baby Bear went home and took the pills every day as Dr. Goldilocks had asked her.

Two weeks later Baby Bear came back to see Dr. Goldilocks. "How do you feel now?" asked Dr. Goldilocks.

Baby Bear said, "I feel much better. My paws are no longer trembling.

My heart is no longer pounding. I don't feel hot anymore, and I have stopped losing weight."

Dr. Goldilocks said to her, "It sounds like your thyroid hormone level is exactly where it should be:

Not too **LOW**, not too **HIGH**, but **JUST RIGHT**.

You should continue the same medicine. In the future, we may give you a different treatment with a special type of iodine called iodine-131, which will permanently reduce the hormone produced by the thyroid."

A few days later Papa Bear came to see Dr. Goldilocks.

"How do you feel, Papa Bear?" Dr. Goldilocks asked.

Papa Bear said, "I feel a lump in my neck.

Sometime the lump hurts.

Sometimes I have trouble swallowing.

I feel pressure in my neck when I turn my head to one side."

Dr. Goldilocks examined Papa Bear.

Dr. Goldilocks said, "Your thyroid is much bigger than it should be.

I can feel some small lumps on your thyroid and one very large lump on the bottom of the left side of the thyroid.

The ultrasound gives us a clear picture of these lumps on your thyroid.

We call this a MULTINODULAR GOITER with a large left THYROID NODULE."

"What can you do to make me feel better?" Papa Bear asked.

Dr. Goldilocks said, "Because the thyroid is very large, and the nodules are causing pressure in your neck, you need an operation to remove the large thyroid gland and the nodules."

Papa Bear went to the hospital to have an operation on his thyroid by Dr. Goldilocks.

She gave him an anesthetic so that he would fall asleep and not feel any pain during the operation.

Dr. Goldilocks removed the whole thyroid including the large nodule.

When the operation was over and Papa Bear woke up, she gave him some thyroid hormone pills to start taking when he went home because he no longer had a thyroid gland to produce his own thyroid hormone.

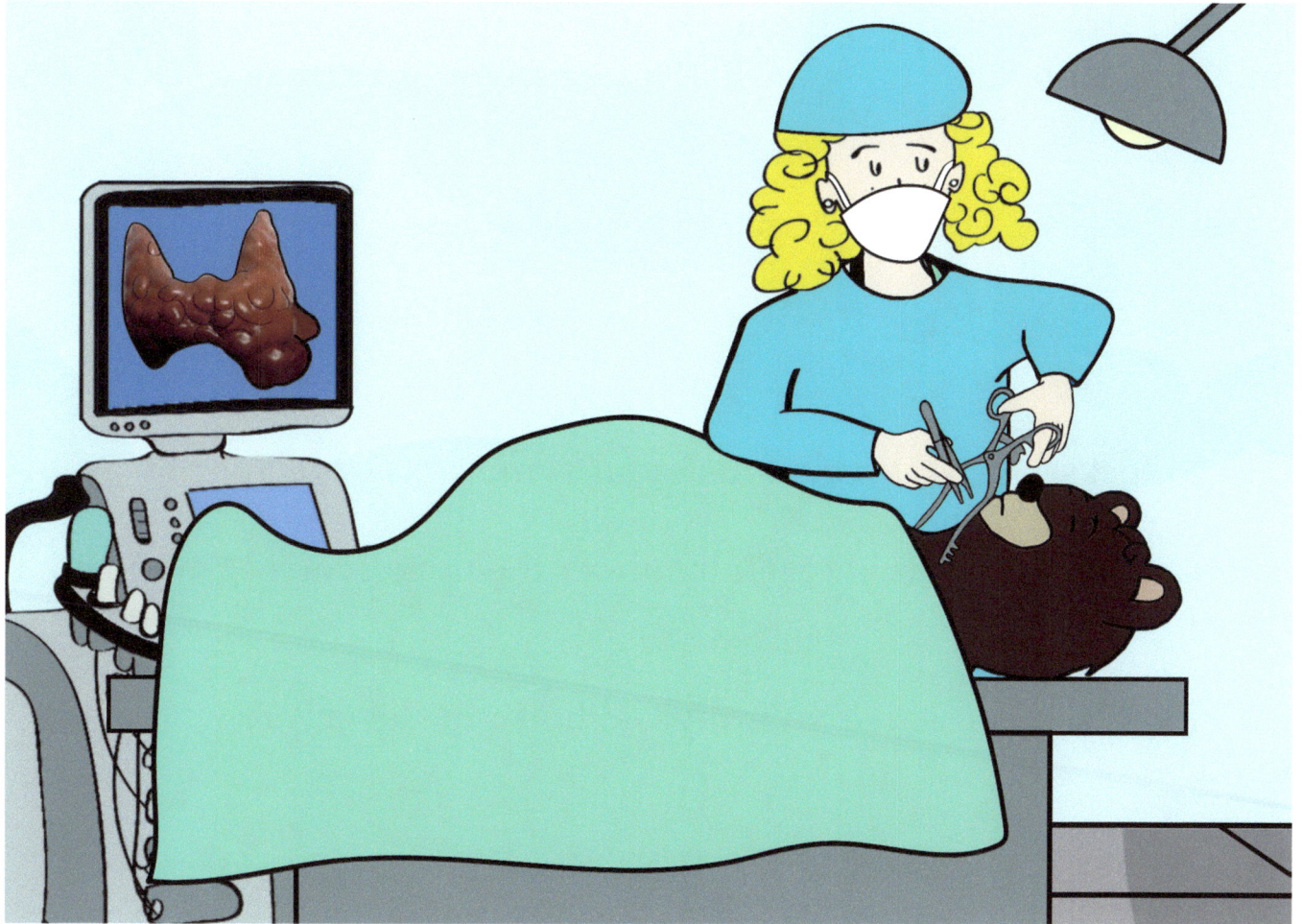

Papa Bear took the thyroid hormone pills for the next month and then went to the laboratory for some blood tests before returning to Dr. Goldilocks' office.

Dr. Goldilocks asked him, "How do you feel now?"

Papa Bear replied, "I feel fine now. I do not feel any more pressure in my neck."

Dr. Goldilocks said, "I am glad that your symptoms have gone away.

We looked at your thyroid carefully under the microscope. You do not have cancer.

Your blood tests show that your thyroid hormone levels are where they should be:

Not too **LOW**, not too **HIGH**, but **JUST RIGHT**."

The Three Bears lived happily ever after because Dr. Goldilocks had treated their thyroid conditions.

They learned why it is important to see an endocrinologist like Dr. Goldilocks when a bear has a thyroid problem.

GLOSSARY

Endocrinologist--a doctor who treats patients with disorders of the endocrine glands including diabetes and diseases of the thyroid gland, the parathyroid glands, the adrenal glands, the pituitary gland, the ovaries, and the testes

Goiter--an enlarged thyroid gland

Hyperthyroidism--- a medical condition caused by having too much thyroid hormone

Hypothyroidism--a medical condition caused by having not enough thyroid hormone

Iodine--a chemical element necessary for thyroid hormone production that is found in saltwater fish, shellfish, sea salt, eggs, poultry, bakery products, seaweed, and kelp

Iodine 131--a radioactive form of iodine used to treat overactive thyroid glands

Methimazole--an oral medicine that reduces the production of thyroid hormone by the thyroid gland

Thyroid Antibodies--molecules produced by the immune system that can cause the thyroid to produce too much or not enough thyroid hormone

Thyroid Gland--a small, butterfly-shaped organ located at the base of the neck that secretes thyroid hormone directly into the blood stream

Thyroid Hormone--a small molecule produced by the thyroid gland that controls the rates of many body processes such as basal metabolic rate and heat production

Thyroid Nodule--a round, oval, or irregularly shaped growth in the thyroid gland that is usually benign, but may be a cancer in some patients

Thyroid Stimulating Hormone--the brain hormone that stimulates the thyroid to make thyroid hormone

Ultrasound--a machine that uses sound waves to produce a picture of the thyroid gland and other organs in the body

THE END

www.ingramcontent.com/pod-product-compliance
Lightning Source LLC
Chambersburg PA
CBHW042100040426
42448CB00002B/83